LUMPIA

by Richard Sebra

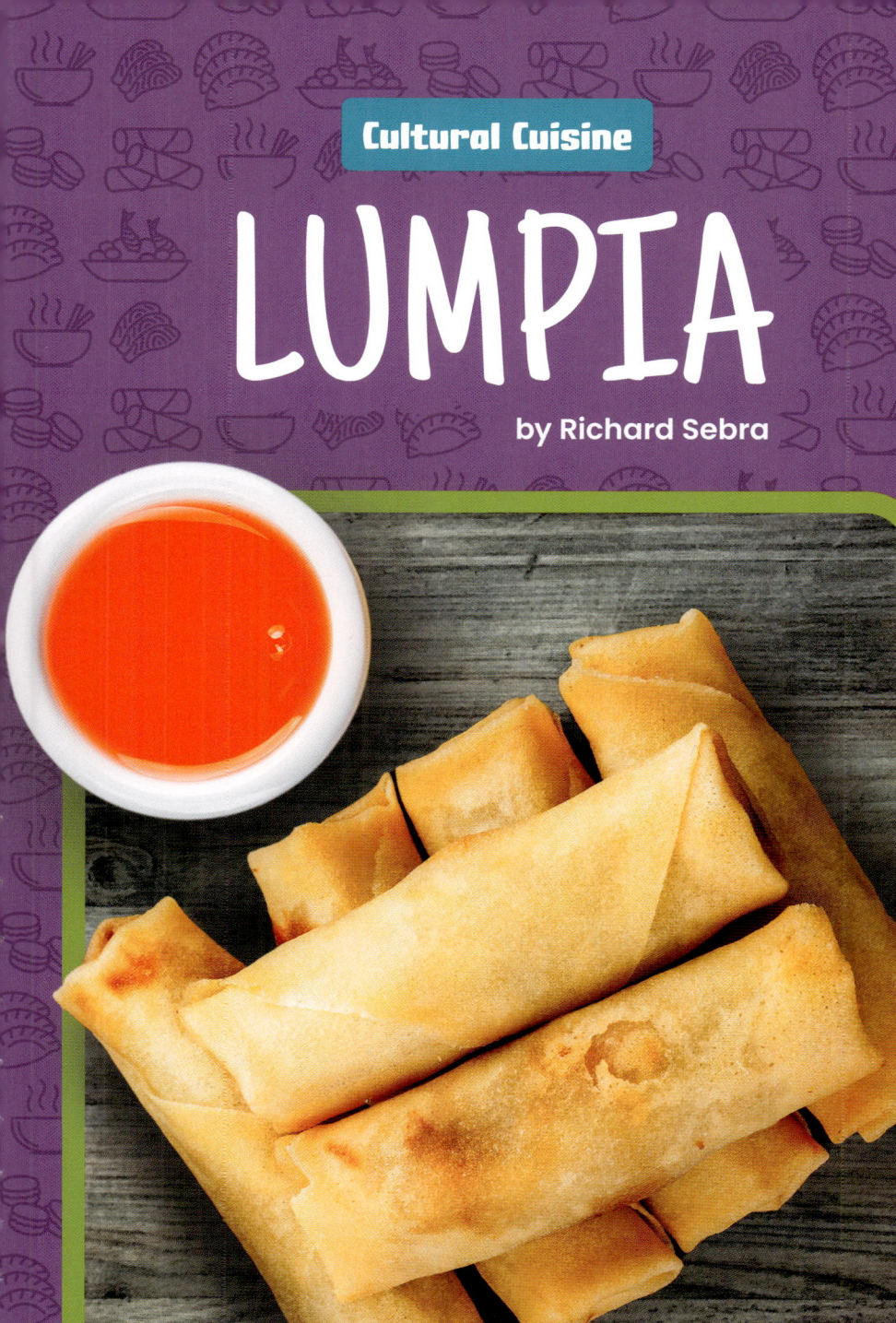

abdobooks.com

Published by Pop!, a division of ABDO, PO Box 398166, Minneapolis, Minnesota 55439. Copyright © 2021 by POP, LLC. International copyrights reserved in all countries. No part of this book may be reproduced in any form without written permission from the publisher. Pop!™ is a trademark and logo of POP, LLC.

Printed in the United States of America, North Mankato, Minnesota.

082020
012021

THIS BOOK CONTAINS RECYCLED MATERIALS

Cover Photo: Shutterstock Images, foreground; iStockphoto, background
Interior Photos: Shutterstock Images, 1 (foreground), 6, 15, 17, 18, 19, 21, 22, 23, 28; iStockphoto, 1 (background), 7, 9, 11, 12, 13, 16, 20, 25, 26–27, 29; danilo pinzon, jr/Alamy, 5, 10

Editor: Sophie Geister-Jones
Series Designers: Candice Keimig, Victoria Bates, and Laura Graphenteen

Library of Congress Control Number: 2019955008

Publisher's Cataloging-in-Publication Data

Names: Sebra, Richard, author.

Title: Lumpia / by Richard Sebra.

Description: Minneapolis, Minnesota : POP!, 2021 | Series: Cultural cuisine | Includes online resources and index.

Identifiers: ISBN 9781532167751 (lib. bdg.) | ISBN 9781532168857 (ebook)

Subjects: LCSH: Cooking, Indonesian--Juvenile literature. | Fried food--Juvenile literature. | Ethnic food--Juvenile literature. | International cooking--Juvenile literature. | Food--Social aspects--Juvenile literature.

Classification: DDC 641.59595--dc23

WELCOME TO DiscoverRoo!

Pop open this book and you'll find QR codes loaded with information, so you can learn even more!

Scan this code* and others like it while you read, or visit the website below to make this book pop!

popbooksonline.com/lumpia

*Scanning QR codes requires a web-enabled smart device with a QR code reader app and a camera.

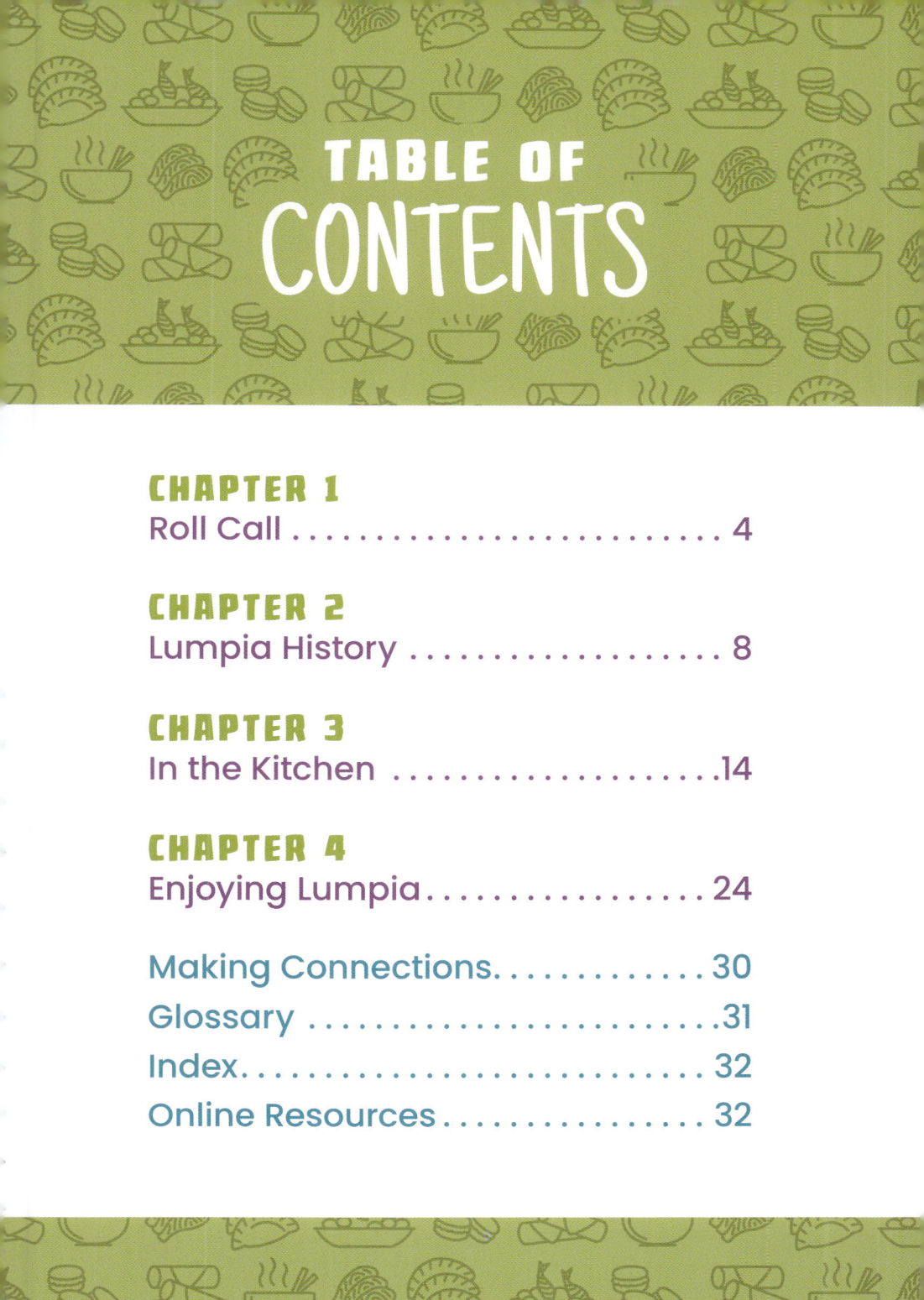

TABLE OF
CONTENTS

CHAPTER 1

ROLL CALL

A woman stands over a pan of hot oil.

She is making lumpia. The woman places

rolls filled with meat and vegetables into

the pan. She fries them until they are

crispy. Then she moves them to a paper

WATCH A
VIDEO HERE!

Lumpia can be sold from food trucks or stands on the side of the street.

towel to cool and dry. Soon the towel is

covered with golden-brown rolls.

Lumpia wrappers are made from a pastry dough. They become crispy when fried.

Lumpia is a type of spring roll. It is a common party food in the Philippines. There are many ways to enjoy lumpia. Some people eat fried lumpia filled with

pork. Other people eat fresh, uncooked

lumpia filled with vegetables.

DID YOU KNOW?

Lumpia is pronounced LOOM-pee-uh.

Fresh lumpia use a different wrapper than fried lumpia.
It is softer and thicker.

CHAPTER 2

LUMPIA HISTORY

Lumpia is a famous **Filipino** dish. But it got its start in China. Travelers from China came to the Philippines in the 600s. They brought spring rolls with them. The rolls had a filling of meat and vegetables inside a crispy crust.

COMPLETE AN ACTIVITY HERE!

Spring rolls have a thicker wrapper than lumpia. They are fried differently as well.

Gradually, these rolls developed into lumpia. Spring rolls and lumpia have similar fillings. But lumpia have a slightly different shape. They are thinner and longer. This shape comes from their wrappers. Lumpia wrappers are very thin. In addition, they are **precooked**. These changes made lumpia a dish of its own.

FOOD TRAVELS

China and the Philippines are close to each other. Their cultures have many similarities, including foods like lumpia and spring rolls.

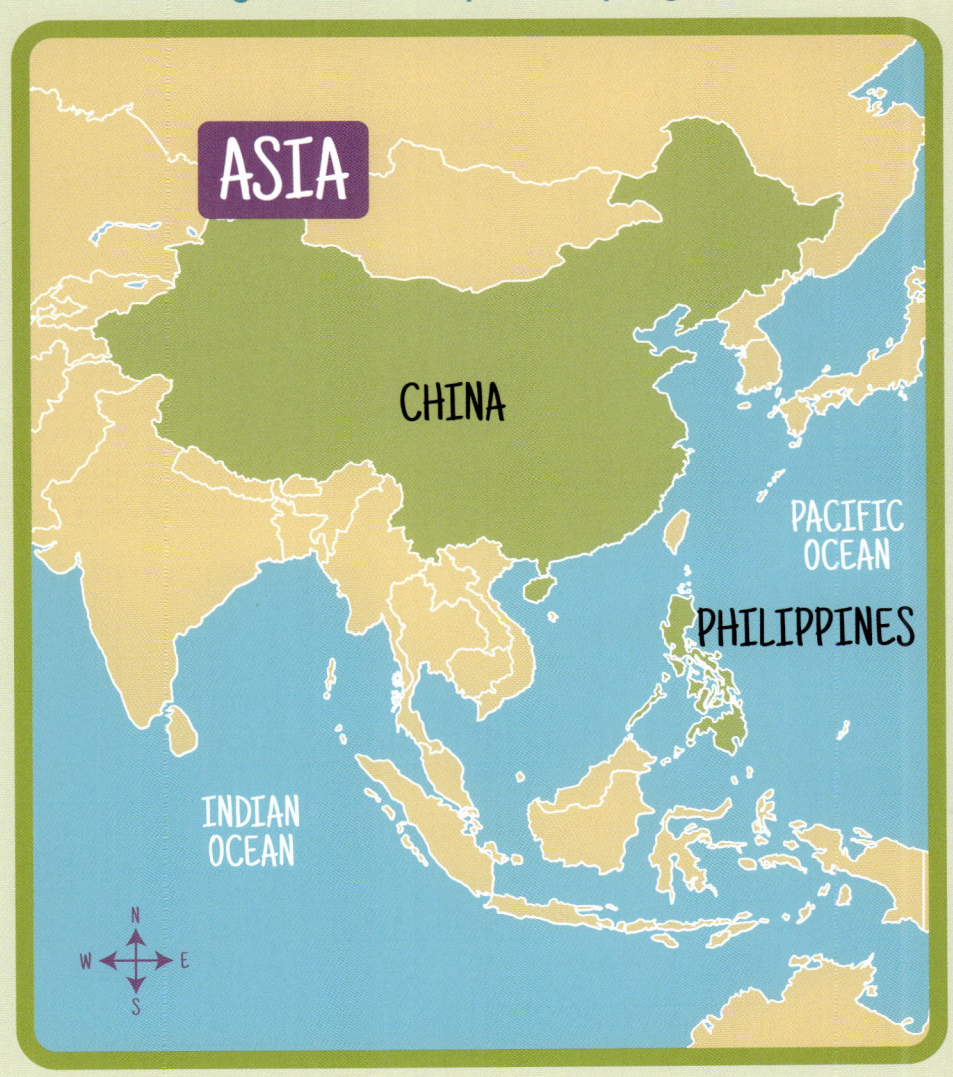

ASIA

CHINA

PACIFIC OCEAN

PHILIPPINES

INDIAN OCEAN

N
W — E
S

Spanish influence is visible in some of the buildings in the Philippines.

Lumpia is also influenced by Spanish **cuisine**. Spain ruled the Philippines from 1565 to 1898. During this time, Spain spread its ideas and practices to the islands of the Philippines. People blended

Spanish and Filipino flavors.

CHAPTER 3

IN THE KITCHEN

Many lumpia recipes exist. But they are all prepared in the same way. The filling is made first. It contains ground pork, vegetables, and spices. The meat is often cooked in the **adobo** style.

TRY A RECIPE HERE!

Pork and chicken are common meat choices for the adobo style of cooking.

After spooning in the filling, the cook wets the lumpia wrapper to seal it shut.

Next, the lumpia must be wrapped.

Lumpia wrappers are made from flour

and water. Cooks add filling to a flat

wrapper. Then they roll it up into a

tube shape.

The rolled lumpia are dropped into a pan of hot oil. The oil fries the wrapper and heats the filling. Lumpia do not take long to cook. After five or six minutes, they are crispy and ready to eat.

Lumpia are not completely covered in oil when they fry. They sit in a shallow pan.

Most fresh lumpia rolls do not have any meat in them.

Fresh lumpia are not fried. Their filling

is not usually cooked either. Instead,

people chop fresh vegetables. They roll

them in a wrapper. This kind of lumpia is

often served cold.

Dinamita *are fried before they are served.*

Dessert lumpia are sometimes served with chocolate dipping sauce.

Lumpia can even be a dessert.

These lumpia are fried. They have sweet

fillings. Turon is a dessert made with

lumpia wrappers and fruit. Jackfruit and banana are common fillings for dessert lumpia. But turon can also be filled with mango or even sweet potato.

Bananas are rolled in brown sugar before being wrapped and fried to make turon.

RECIPE CHECKLIST

LUMPIA INGREDIENTS

- 6 ounces cabbage
- 5 garlic cloves
- 1 inch peeled ginger
- 2 pounds ground pork
- 2 tablespoons soy sauce
- 2 eggs
- 3 dashes black pepper
- 30 lumpia wrappers
- oil 1/2 inch deep in pan

Makes 30 lumpia

INSTRUCTIONS

1. Chop the cabbage, garlic, and ginger.

2. Combine all ingredients except the wrappers and oil. Mix in a bowl.

3. Cut the wrappers into rectangles.

4. Dampen the wrappers so they are easy to bend.

5. Place a spoonful of filling on one edge of the wrapper.

6. Roll the lumpia.

7. Add oil to a pan on the stove. Heat it up.

8. Fry the lumpia in the oil.

CHAPTER 4

ENJOYING LUMPIA

Lumpia are a common **street food** in the Philippines. **Vendors** fry lumpia ahead of time. Then they sell them out of a covered pan or box. The delicious treats tend to sell out quickly.

LEARN MORE HERE!

Lumpia are easy to eat without a plate or silverware.

Lumpia are also popular at **Filipino** gatherings. Often, families pass down their own recipes. They bring these

Lumpia is one of the most popular snacks in Indonesia.

traditions with them wherever they live.

People around the world enjoy many

versions of this tasty treat.

Indonesia has its own version of lumpia. Indonesian lumpia are filled with bamboo shoots, eggs, and chicken or shrimp.

Lumpia can be eaten plain. But they

are often served with a dipping sauce.

There are many different recipes

for lumpia.

There are many

different sauces too.

And people keep

exploring new ways

to enjoy lumpia.

LOTS OF SAUCES

Dipping sauce is an important part of eating lumpia. People have many sauces to choose from. Some people use sweet and sour sauce. Others use a mix of soy sauce and vinegar. In the Philippines, banana ketchup is a common choice. It is made with bananas, sugar, and vinegar.

MAKING CONNECTIONS

TEXT-TO-SELF

Would you rather eat fresh lumpia or fried lumpia? Why?

TEXT-TO-TEXT

Have you read other books about food that is fried? How is that food similar to lumpia? How is it different?

TEXT-TO-WORLD

Lumpia are often served at celebrations in the Philippines. What other foods do people commonly eat at celebrations?

GLOSSARY

adobo — a cooking style in which meat is cooked with vinegar, soy sauce, and garlic.

cuisine — a style of cooking, especially as connected to a specific country.

Filipino — from the Philippines.

precooked — already partly or fully cooked.

street food — prepared food sold on the street to be eaten immediately.

tradition — a belief or way of doing things that is passed down from person to person over time.

vendors — people who sell things.

INDEX

ONLINE RESOURCES
popbooksonline.com

Scan this code* and others like it while you read, or visit the website below to make this book pop!

popbooksonline.com/lumpia

*Scanning QR codes requires a web-enabled smart device with a QR code reader app and a camera.